CAROL HEISS

OLYMPIC
QUEEN

CAROL HEISS

OLYMPIC QUEEN ⊕⊕⊕

by Robert Parker

A Signal Book
Doubleday & Company, Inc.
Garden City, New York

Other Signal Books

PONY OF THE SIOUX
THE JUNGLE SECRET
BONNIE
NORTH POLE

text based on GOLDEN SKATES by Helen Bolstad

contents

CAROL HEISS

OLYMPIC QUEEN

Squaw Valley, California, where the 1960 Winter Olympics took place

1

A dream come true

The music began to play. A hush fell over the great skating rink at Squaw Valley.

"Here she comes!" someone whispered.

A slim blonde girl in a short skater's costume glided out onto the ice. For a second she paused, then she whirled away, leaping and spinning.

An excited hum ran through the watching crowd. The girl's speed increased. The blades of her figure skates flashed across the ice. Through a great window at one end of the ice rink the flags of more than thirty nations could be seen in the afternoon sun, but the people on either side of the rink saw only the small figure, wonderful and alone, skating across the ice.

Her name was Carol Heiss, and this was the high

point of her career—the 1960 Winter Olympic Games. Thousands of eyes followed her quick, doll-like figure around the ice. She leaped and spun. People held their breath.

"Wonderful! Wonderful!" someone whispered.

Surely, she moved through the difficult patterns. It was like a dance. She flashed past television cameras working to keep up with her. In millions of homes all over the country people were watching her.

At the side of the great rink nine men and women sat quietly. They were the judges, and they never took their eyes off her. Each move she made they checked. They must judge her fairly.

Far across the country, in Queens, New York, another man sat silent and still in front of his television set. He was Edward Heiss, Carol's father. His hands closed hard on the arms of his chair. He leaned forward, watching. Great excitement rose up in him. He could not help his daughter now. He could only watch. But with each spin she made, each glide and quick turn, his prayers went out to her.

"God be with you," he said quietly.

Four brief minutes! That was all the time she was allowed, and in those few minutes fifteen years of work and sacrifice, of hopes and triumphs and disappointments would reach their greatest test. As Carol's father watched, he could not think of a more beautiful, happy ending for the story of those years.

The music swelled. Carol spun into a final wonderful series of flashing figures. Her small body arched. For one last second she stood still, arms upstretched, and then it was over.

"Perfect. Perfect."

Cheers broke from the crowd. People were clapping, shouting. And then everyone was quiet. The judges were walking out onto the ice, their faces telling nothing. Had Carol won? People waited eagerly.

One by one, the judges held their score cards high. At the edge of the rink, Carol's coach, Pierre Brunet, added the numbers to Carol's score. But the audience did not wait to hear. Carol had done it! People stood and cheered her, making wave after wave of sound. In the flood of cheering, Carol's tiny figure disappeared from the rink.

At home her father bowed his head. "Carol, you have won," he said out loud. "You are the first American to win a gold medal at the 1960 Games." Great pride filled his heart, yet sadness came to him, too. Carol's mother was not alive to share in this moment of triumph, and he remembered how she had believed it *must* happen, how she had longed to see it.

Back at the ice rink, Carol was being led to the winner's platform. Four years ago, it had seemed as tall as a mountain to her, but now she climbed the steps and stood, slim and straight, while the excitement increased around her. She lifted her head, and

At Squaw Valley, Carol won the first Gold Medal
that was given to any American. Here she talks on
TV with the CBS announcer Walter Cronkite

A moment Carol will always remember: coming home to New York where Mayor Wagner gave Carol the city's gold medal

tears filled her eyes. She seemed to be looking far, far off into the distance, and in her heart she whispered: "It is for you, Mother. I promised."

During the next days Carol was swept into a world of excitement. People wanted her to sign her name. Talent scouts from the movies and television wanted her to sign contracts. Newspapermen wanted the story of her life.

In Washington, D.C., Congressman John V. Lindsay made a speech about her. "It is refreshing," he said, "to have someone like Carol Heiss set such high standards of courage and strength for our youth to follow."

Carol was the Queen of America. When she arrived in New York, 250,000 people crowded along Broadway to welcome her. Clouds of paper streamers fluttered around her. On the steps of City Hall, the Mayor gave her a medal. "To Carol Heiss," it read. "Figure skater extraordinary, inspiration to our youth, admired daughter of New York."

Who is this girl who made good? What is she like? Is there another story behind the big story in the newspapers? Many things have been written about her. Some reports have told of quarrels with other skaters. Some have told of her promise to her dying mother, her future plans.

But the real Carol is not the Carol of the news stories. Hers is more than just a Cinderella story. Her story is best told through the people who have known her—those she lived with, played with, practiced with, studied with, and skated against. They have known this champion in the dressing room, in the classroom, at parties, and on the ice.

The place to start? It is in her home, among her family. They are the ones who have known her best.

It all began . . .

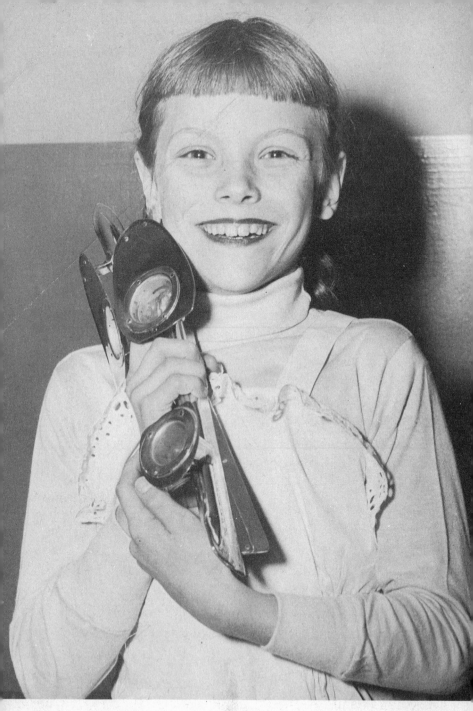

At nine, Carol won her first silver skates in the Girls' Midget finals

2

The beginning

You might say it all began with a tooth that ached. But that is a long way from the whole story.

Over in Munich, Germany, a young man dreamed of coming to America. His name was Edward Heiss. He had learned to be a baker and there were jobs he could have, but he felt there was no future for him in his own country.

He did not have very much money—not nearly enough to pay his way clear to America, but he made up his mind. He packed his bags, said goodbye to his parents, and set out. First he went to Switzerland and worked there, saving his money. Then he went to Italy, and then to France. Finally the great day came. He had saved enough money. He hurried to the steamship company and got his ticket. Then he set sail for the United States.

Here in America he did not have trouble finding work, for he was a very good baker indeed. But he had not been here long when a tooth began to ache.

There was only one thing to do: Go to a dentist. Edward did not know any dentists in this country, but he picked one out and went.

The dentist looked into his mouth. He shook his head. "That tooth will have to be filled," he said.

When the dentist finished work, they talked. "I come from Munich," Edward said.

The dentist looked surprised. "Munich!" he said, and then his eyes twinkled. "You must come to my home for dinner. There is someone from Germany there whom I want you to meet."

A date was set. Edward was excited. He wondered who it could be from his homeland that he would meet. He dressed carefully, putting on his best suit, and when the night came he was right on time.

It was a wonderful evening. The dinner was excellent—all the home dishes he had been missing. But to tell the truth, Edward did not pay quite as much attention to the dinner as he might have. For the "someone" the dentist had wanted him to meet was a very pretty young girl named Marie. Edward could hardly take his eyes off her.

That first visit to the dentist's home was not to be

the last one. He began to call frequently. The dentist's eyes twinkled more than ever, and his wife nodded and smiled. "This is going to be a very good thing," she told him. As for Marie, she knew she had fallen in love, and her eyes were shining.

"Oh, Edward is a wonderful man," she admitted.

In 1936, Edward and Marie were married. They were very happy. They bought a house in Ozone Park, near New York City, and they loved the tree-lined streets, the parks, and the beaches of Long Island Sound. They were only fifteen miles from the heart of New York City, and this was exciting, too.

Four happy years went by, and then to add to their happiness, their first baby was born. Her birthday was January 20, 1940, and they named her Carol. Never, they thought, had there been such a beautiful baby. But then on November 19, 1942, Nancy was born, and she was just as beautiful to them. Two years later, on September 5, Bruce arrived, a strong, handsome baby.

The house in Ozone Park was filled with children's laughter and play. Marie Heiss hurried about, taking care of them all.

"The children are almost too full of energy," she wrote to her mother. "I may have to find something to keep them busy."

One day when Carol was three and a half, Marie and Edward were shopping. In a store where they

Determined young Carol did something unheard of—entered

had stopped, they saw a tiny pair of roller skates. Marie caught at Edward's arm.

"Look!" she cried. "They are just Carol's size!"

The picture of tiny, blonde Carol spinning around on roller skates was suddenly too much for them to resist. They bought the skates and started home.

They were only halfway there when Carol's mother began to worry. "She is so little!" she said.

"But she is very quick," her father put in.

"I would never dare let her go on the sidewalk with

a speed skating race—and won it wearing her figure skates!

skates! It is too dangerous. She's not four years old."

That was right. Carol's father agreed at once. But they had bought the present. What would they do? And then Edward's face cleared. "I have it!" he cried. "She can skate in the basement."

They could hardly wait to get home, and Carol's eyes danced when she saw the present.

Her father caught her up. Together he and Marie carried her down to the basement. Carol bounced on Mother's lap as her father fitted the tiny skates.

They set little Carol on her feet. At first she slipped and slid, and her father held her up. Then suddenly she found her balance. She broke away from his hands. She was skating!

"I can't believe it!" Marie gasped, wide-eyed.

"Only three and a half!" her father exclaimed.

Carol laughed with glee. It was just as though she had been born to skate.

Marie and Edward watched in silence. Then Marie put her hand on Edward's. "She has perfect balance," she whispered, and they both were silent for they knew that perfect balance was something very, very few people have. Carol was one of them.

The rest of that summer, the noise of Carol's roller skates filled the house. Winter came. Edward and Marie looked at each other, a question in their eyes.

"She is unusual," Edward said.

"I think she should have lessons," Marie said. And Edward did, too.

A few days later, Carol's mother took her to an ice-skating rink where there was a teacher. The teacher looked down at tiny Carol with a frown. "She is very young," he said.

"Just try her," Marie begged.

It was the custom to pay the teacher before any lesson was given, and Marie held out the money. After a moment, the teacher took it.

Marie laced on Carol's new ice skates. When Carol

was ready, she called the teacher. But before the teacher could get across the ice, Carol had jumped up. For a second she balanced, getting the feel of the single-bladed skates. Then she was off, gliding about the ice as free as a bird, her blonde curls flying.

Without a word the teacher watched. Carol made a graceful turn. The teacher turned to Marie. He held out the money. "I can't teach your child anything," he said. "Here is your money back."

Now Marie and Edward knew for sure that they must find a teacher for Carol. It was going to take money, and with three mouths to feed and the house to keep up, they did not have very much left over. But a teacher was found.

There came the time for an exciting ice show in Brooklyn. The Figure Skating Club gave the show, and they wanted Carol to be in it. She wasn't even big enough to go to school yet, but Marie and Edward decided she could be in the show.

The night came. Marie and Edward sat in the audience, hoping they had made the right decision. Skaters in beautiful costumes glided onto the ice. They went through their steps, and the crowd clapped.

"Oh, Edward!" Marie whispered. "She is so *little*!"

"She will do all right," Carol's father said.

A great box was carried onto the ice. It looked like a gift. Other skaters circled around it, showing that they wondered what could be inside.

Then the box was opened. Out of it jumped Carol in her pretty costume. Around the rink she skated like a little doll, doing a waltz step. The crowd clapped and cheered. Carol smiled happily. She passed the place where her mother and father sat, and she almost waved! Just in time she remembered that she was in a show and must not wave to her parents. But as soon as it was over, when her Daddy caught her up in his arms, she cried:

"I saw you! I saw you!"

That night, after Carol and her little sister and brother were asleep, Marie and Edward sat talking.

"We must find her better teachers," Marie said.

"That's right," Edward nodded. "I have heard about the Junior Figure Skating Club of New York. They say it is very good."

"Then that is where she will go!" Marie said. Her eyes flew to her husband's. "It is very expensive."

"We were going to buy a car this year," Edward said. "But we both know we can do without it. The money will pay for her lessons."

The Junior Figure Skating Club had two wonderful teachers. Their names were Pierre and Andrée Brunet, and they had both been Olympic champions. Now they were married and teaching young skaters.

Marie took Carol to them. They watched her skate, and then accepted her as a pupil. Andrée would teach her first. Pierre, her husband, took only the very best.

Carol fell in love with both the Brunets. She wanted to be just like them, especially Andrée. "When I grow up I am going to be the world's champion figure skater!" she announced proudly.

It was a very big ambition, but as the days went by Carol talked about it more and more. One day Carol ran in from play with a little friend.

"I want a kitty," she said. It seemed her friend had just been given a new kitten. "Mama, please!"

"Let me see," her mother joked. "When you get to be the world champion figure skater you are always talking about, I will get you a pure alley cat."

Carol didn't see that it was a joke. She danced away singing: "I'm going to have a kitty! I am going to have a kitty!"

The next day at school, she told all the other children what her mother had said. The biggest boy in the class laughed. "Alley cat!" he said. "What is so wonderful about a plain, ordinary old cat? I bet you never win it *or* the world's championship!"

Carol was too hurt to tell her mother. The only other person who might understand was her skating teacher, and she told her, sobbing.

Andrée wiped away her tears. "Alley cats can be beautiful," she said. "And maybe you will win the championship, too. Now let me see you skate. It will make you that much closer to winning."

Carol and Nancy liked nothing better than in-pairs skating

3

The heart of a champion

Carol started to learn the things a good figure skater must know how to do, and must practice until she can do them perfectly. She learned them so rapidly that one day when Marie brought her to the rink, Pierre and Andrée had a serious talk with her mother.

"We have never seen a child with so much ability," Andrée said.

"What is more," Pierre added, "she has the heart of a champion. She has nerve. She never gives up."

Andrée leaned forward. "We believe that if she studies hard, in ten years she can be champion of the world!"

Marie caught her breath. It was one thing to call six-year-old Carol "Champ," the way they did around the house; it was quite another to have professional coaches tell her that Carol could *be* champion. She felt suddenly frightened.

"It is impossible," she said.

"Why?" Pierre asked. "Ten years from now some skater must win. Right now that skater is about Carol's age. Why shouldn't the winner ten years from now be Carol?"

Carol's mother hadn't thought of it that way. She had always pictured an Olympic champion as someone grown-up, but now she realized that in ten years Carol would be nearly grown.

"But—it is so impossible," she murmured, still trying to get used to the idea.

"Everyone has to have a goal," Pierre Brunet said. "Something to work for. We are training our own son to be an Olympic champion. It is a fine goal for Carol, too."

And so the decision was made. Carol and her mother and father agreed. From this time on, she would work to become champion of the world.

Carol was so excited with the idea that she began to lose interest in everything else. She didn't think about her friends. Her school marks went down. One day, when she came home from school with a poor mark in arithmetic, she tried an excuse.

"But, Mama, I don't *like* arithmetic."

"Don't you?" her mother said. "What a shame.

Though Carol, older, had more trophies than Nancy,
neither sister was ever jealous, no matter who won

When you have a little girl of your own, how will you
ever be able to decide whether or not you can buy her
a new dress?"

"But that is different!" Carol protested.

"Oh, no," her mother said. "Your father and I use
arithmetic every day to find out what we can pay for
—our food and clothes and your lessons. We have
to take the amount your father earns, and take from
it the cost of each thing we pay for. That is arithmetic. Come on, we will try it."

They did a few sums. Carol found that they were
not hard at all, once she tried them.

"That is fine," her mother said. "See how it goes?

No wonder the "golden kids" were so popular! They skated

happily with each other or with older, more advanced skaters

Just be careful. You can't be in a hurry. And you can't be lazy. There is no excuse for either."

"No, Mother," Carol said, feeling a little ashamed.

"Someone has to get the A's, doesn't she?" her mother said. "I want it to be you."

Carol thought of how Pierre had said someone must be world champion, and he thought she could be—if she worked. It was the same in school.

That night when her father came home, he heard what had happened. He looked at Carol seriously. "Skating is all right, Carol," he said. "We want you to do your best. But remember that an education counts. With a good education, you can be anything."

Carol studied harder after that. Her report card showed A's. At school some of the other children began calling her "teacher's pet." One girl, especially, teased her.

"I don't like her!" Carol cried to her mother. "Why does she have to be so bad?"

"Maybe it is because she doesn't really know you," her mother said. "And maybe you don't know her well enough, either. Why don't you bring her home to play after school tomorrow?"

"To play? Here with me? After what she said?" Carol protested.

But her mother kept saying it was a good idea, and finally Carol gave in. The next day she invited the little girl home. They were both feeling shy when they came in. Carol's mother gave them milk and cookies, but still they did not know what to do.

Carol's mother noticed the little girl looking at the pictures on the wall. Mrs. Heiss liked to paint, and she had done some of the pictures. She smiled at her. "Do you like to draw?" she asked.

The girl nodded eagerly.

"Then let's draw," Mrs. Heiss smiled. She led the two little girls out onto the sun porch where her drawing table was. "Here are my paints," she said. "Shall we see what each of us can do?"

Mr. Heiss had to get supper that night. The others were still painting. Finally, the little girl went home and Carol went to bed. As her mother tucked her in, Carol looked up at her.

"She paints better than I do," she said.

Her mother smiled. "Now you have discovered that other people have talents, too. They may be different from yours, but that doesn't make them any less interesting, does it?"

Carol pulled up the bed covers around her. "No, Mama, it doesn't," she agreed. She sighed happily.

Her mother smiled. Every day that Carol learned more about skating, she was learning more about other things, too. And Carol's mother and father wanted just that. They wanted her to be ready for life, as her coach wanted her to be ready for the careful eyes of the judges when the time came.

Carol enjoyed Christmas on the ice while preparing for first world mee

4

Figure skating

Every day Carol went to her skating lesson. Every day, it seemed, Andrée had something new for her to learn.

"Oh, Mama!" Carol cried, "I have to do so many things."

Her mother smiled. "Everyone does," she said, "if he wants to achieve anything."

Carol was learning that skating took grace, strength, speed, form and courage. It was more than just gliding around the ice while people exclaimed: "Isn't she simply wonderful!"

Her coach taught her that there are two kinds of skating. One is called free skating, and it is just what it says. In it a skater does a series of jumps, spins and loops of his own choice. He can make them as difficult as he wants—but the rules say he must skate to music, and the performance must last just so long, usually four minutes.

The other kind of skating is called school figures. These are the ABC's of figure skating. Just as a little girl in first grade learns that letters make up words, and words make sentences, so Carol learned that the school figures a skater does are the basis of everything else.

Each figure is some form of the figure 8. Carol learned that national skating associations in every country say just how these school figures must be performed. In the United States, it is the United States Figure Skating Association that decides; in Canada it is the Canadian Figure Skating Association, and each one is very strict. School figures must be performed perfectly to get a top score.

Each morning Carol practiced her school figures on her "patch" of ice. Ice patches are like a group of squares marked off on the rink, and each skater rents his own where he can practice.

Every day Andrée Brunet worked with Carol. She showed her how to do loops and brackets and counters—all of them part of the figure 8.

"Mama!" Carol cried one day. "There are sixty-two types of school figures I have to learn!"

Her mother smiled. "You can do it," she said.

"And when you do, you will be on your way to being a real champion."

"Why do I have to learn so many?" Carol protested to her teacher.

"Because," Andrée Brunet said, "when you are skating in competition, you never know until the last minute which skating figures you will be asked to perform. So you have to know them all. Now come on, Carol, practice!"

And Carol practiced. She learned that each tracing her skates made on the ice was important. It must fall exactly over the previous line she had made if it was to count. She learned that the outside and inside of her skate blades made different patterns on the ice, and that the judges would look to see if she had used the correct side.

Practice! Practice! Practice! The same things over and over!

"I want to do something new!" Carol cried. "What fun is it doing the same old things?"

"It is *no* fun," her teacher said. "The reason we do things over and over is to get them right. Do you think you can do something once and have it be perfect?"

Carol had to admit that she could not.

The day was drawing near when official tests would be given by the Skating Club. If Carol wanted to stay in the Club, she would have to pass these

Carol needed grace, speed and courage to win second place in the 1956 Winter Olympics when she was only 16 years old

tests. They were very difficult. The judges would check to see if she was steady on her feet. They would want to see if she could skate backward and forward equally well. They wanted to know if she could use the blade edges of her skates properly, cutting with the inside edge one time, the outside edge another.

They would ask her to do an inside and an outside circle 8. That meant cutting a figure 8 in just a certain way on the ice. She would have to do a waltz 8—that was another school figure. And she would have to give a free-skating performance.

"That is the part I like best!" Carol cried.

There would be eight tests. If she passed the first three, she would get a nickel medal. If she passed the next four, she would get a silver medal. If she passed the most difficult tests, she would get a gold medal.

Carol was very nervous when the time came for her first test. Most of the skaters who were taking the test were older than she. Her teacher smiled.

"You can do it," she said.

Carol felt her heart flutter as she skated out onto the ice. She began her school figures. The judges watched very carefully. They looked to see if the lines her skates made matched. Carol skated on.

Suddenly the judges were shaking their heads, whispering together.

"Are you sure?" one judge said.

They knew that when she skated a school figure, her skates must trace the pattern she made the second time directly over the first lines she had made. But she was so light, her skates hardly cut the ice!

Never had the judges had such a problem. They peered at the ice. They studied and studied. And finally they decided.

Carol had passed.

It was like graduating from sixth grade in school. Now Carol was ready for more difficult lessons. It was Pierre Brunet who taught the best skaters.

Would he take Carol?

The skater learns at the start that skates have an inside and an outside edge. Rule book tells what forms "school" figures must take. Each is based on figure 8— two circles—and must be skated three times. On this page, Carol shows three stages of a school figure. Opposite, she performs free skating —which consists of unspecified movements to music of her own choice

Start from an outside edge

Going into outside back loop

Pulling out of outside back loop

Simple bunny hop   *Axel Paulsen*

Sit spin   *Inside spread eagle*

At Squaw Valley, Carol practiced five hours every day for her coac

5

Coach Pierre Brunet

Andrée and Pierre Brunet were both very fine skaters. They had won two Olympic gold medals for in-pairs skating. That simply means skating as a team of two. Their first medal they won in the 1929 Games. They repeated their victory at Lake Placid, New York, in 1932.

Each time they had represented their native country, France. Then they decided they would come to the United States and make this their home.

They had one son. His name was Jean-Pierre, which is a name many French boys have, just as many boys in America are called John or Peter.

When he was very little, Jean-Pierre showed talent for skating. His father was sure he could grow up to be a champion, and through the years Jean-Pierre had grown better and better. Now he was almost ready, and his father was spending all his time training his son. He did not want to take any other pupils unless they were very good.

Jean-Pierre liked to practice. He was very athletic, strong and quick. Every day he spent hours with his father on the ice learning the many difficult figures a skater must know. Carol had often seen him on the ice.

Jean-Pierre had a very good skating record. When he had entered his first competition in the beginning class, he defeated another promising young skater named Dick Button.

"He will be Olympic champion some day," his father said proudly. And Andrée agreed.

Andrée knew now that Carol was ready for Pierre's instruction. But Pierre was so busy coaching Jean-Pierre that he could hardly see any other skater. He told his wife that there would be time later.

She talked to Pierre, but he brushed her aside. How could he give time to some little girl when there was so much help he could give his son? Yes, yes—of course he knew that Carol had a future. Hadn't he said so himself? But Andrée could teach her. There was still plenty of time.

And then tragedy came to the Brunet home. It was 1948, and Jean-Pierre was seventeen. He had driven off in a car, and there was a terrible accident. Jean-Pierre was killed.

His father could not believe it had really happened. When he got up in the morning, he could hardly understand that his son would not be there. When he went out on the ice, he almost expected to see Jean-Pierre come skating out to him.

He was in a state of shock. Sometimes he sat on a bench at the side of the rink, his head buried in his hands, and his heart kept crying out for his son. Nothing seemed any good to him now that Jean-Pierre was gone. He didn't want anything more to do with skating.

Andrée was worried. "What can I do?" she asked herself over and over.

If she could only get Pierre interested in teaching Carol! She tried to talk to him, but he would not even listen.

"How can I teach anyone else," he cried, "now that Jean-Pierre is gone!"

Andrée waited her time. Every day that Pierre came to the rink she saw to it that Carol was practicing where he might see her. But Pierre seemed not even to look her way.

Then one day when Pierre was sitting there, Andrée chose a patch of ice right in front of him for Carol's practice. She made Carol go through every one of her school figures, doing her best. At last she saw Pierre glance at her, then begin to watch. Carol tried a more difficult figure. Andrée saw a flash of interest come to his eyes. She held her breath. Was it going to work?

Carol went through two more figures, performing them almost perfectly, though she was only eight. Pierre Brunet leaned forward. Andrée saw him nod as though he were pleased.

Instantly she called to Carol: "That is all for to-day. You may go now."

Carol started to skate away. And just what Andrée had hoped would happen, did happen. Pierre stopped Carol. "Don't go yet! That last figure you did, you are doing one thing wrong. Come here, we will go through it now until you get it right!"

Andrée sighed happily. Pierre would be all right now. His interest had been captured. Now he had something to help replace the loss of his son. *It is a new life beginning for him*, Andrée said silently. *And for Carol.*

In the days that followed, Coach Pierre Brunet's interest in Carol increased. He watched her tiny figure dance lightly on the ice. "She has that spark," he said, "the spark that is necessary for a champion."

He spoke her name in the French way: Ca-*roll*. "Ah," he would say, spreading his hands and raising his shoulders. "Sometimes a mother comes to me, asking how long it will take to make her little daughter a figure skater. How do I know? To be good she must practice at least three hours a day, eight months a year. Even if she has talent, she may be lazy as a snake. But Ca-*roll*! *She* has talent—and she *works*!"

Figure skating is very difficult—even more difficult today than it was twenty-five or thirty years ago when Sonja Henie won the first of her three Olympic titles. "Sonja was a great skater," Pierre Brunet said. "But these kids today—they perform on the ice figures Sonja would not even attempt. They must have

Nancy, Carol and Coach Brunet look at Carol's new skates

real devotion today. If you do not make the grade by ten, you are out. You are finished!"

Carol worked very hard. Every day she practiced while Coach Brunet watched at the Skating Club on the fourth floor of Madison Square Garden.

Every time she thought she had learned something perfectly, Coach Brunet would say: "You are not *thinking* hard enough! Now try it again, and *think* about it."

Carol would try again. She learned to do things over and over until they became second nature to her. Her father smiled at his wife.

"She gets that from you," he said. "You know how to stick to things. Carol is just like you."

"She is like you, too," Carol's mother said. "You know how to be firm about a goal. She has the same drive you have."

And indeed, she was like them both. She was a wonderful pupil. "She never fights against what we plan for her," Coach Brunet said. "The only time she gets angry is at herself when she cannot execute a certain move."

When Carol first began to study under Coach Brunet, she had been frightened, for he was very stern. But she found that he was making her do her very best. If he had been easy on her, she could have got by, but by demanding a great deal of her, he brought out the very best ability she had. This was the mark of a good teacher, Carol understood.

He would never take second best as good enough. When she did something he approved, she felt happy, because she knew she had really achieved something.

Nancy and Bruce were taking lessons now, too, and the skating rink became a second home to them all. Andrée and Pierre Brunet were like a second family. They were Aunt Andrée and Uncle Pierre outside of lessons.

At home Uncle Pierre listened to their troubles and gave them advice. But at the rink he was Coach Brunet. At home they might run to him with their troubles, but if one of them took a spill on the ice, they knew better than to turn to Uncle Pierre for sympathy. He would turn away. "One *does* fall in skating," he would say. And they would have to pick themselves up and skate on. Sympathy was no good for a skater. The best thing, Carol learned, was to be honest with herself.

When she fell it meant she had made a mistake. By admitting the mistake, she could correct it. "When you enter a jump in skating," she said, "there is no backing out. Unless you have everything just right, you fall flat." After facing her mistakes, Carol didn't fall flat very often.

Coach Pierre smiled with satisfaction. Carol was learning the lessons to make her a champion.

Neither Carol nor Nancy ever dreamed of becoming anything but a champi

6

Time to get up

It was 5:30 in the morning. The alarm clock went off with a loud ring. Outside it was snowy and dark, and Carol's mother shivered a little as she dressed and went to wake her daughter.

"Time to get up," she said. "The alarm clock has sounded."

Carol dug down under the warm covers. "I don't want to skate today," she announced, and pulled the covers tighter around her.

"Don't you?" her mother said. "Well, I will be glad to go back to bed and stay there. And tomorrow morning, too. You make up your own mind."

Her mother walked out of the room, and Carol began to think. She thought of the fifteen-mile drive to New York. She thought of how the ice would sparkle, and how her skates would flash across it, cutting the figures on its smooth surface. She thought of Coach Brunet and what new things he might teach her today.

And suddenly she was scrambling from bed. "I am getting up, Mama!" she cried. "I *do* want to go skating!"

Little Nancy was already getting into her clothes, and Carol hurried to catch up with her, while their mother helped Bruce dress and their father fixed breakfast. The Heiss family always tried to reach the rink by seven o'clock. It was good to be early, because the patches of ice each skater rented cost less this early in the morning. Then, too, there were fewer skaters who would get up so early, and sometimes the children had the rink all to themselves.

Nancy and Carol looked like little blonde dolls with gray-green eyes. Carol was ahead of Nancy in training, of course, but it was not long before Nancy was better at school figures. Carol liked free skating best. She liked to race across the ice and try trick jumps and spins.

But Coach Brunet knew how important the school figures were. In a competition they were worth 60% of a skater's final score. He was very strict with Carol, especially on those days when she could not seem to master a movement he wished to teach her.

"Again!" he would say. "Now do it again!"

"I can't!" Carol cried sometimes, upset and discouraged. She ran to her mother. But her mother did not wipe away her tears.

"You don't have to do the figure over if you don't want to," she said. "If you don't want to learn, take off your skates, and we will go home. I can think of a lot of other things to do every morning."

Carol bit her lip. It was just like getting up on a cold morning. She had to make up her own mind. She looked across the ice where Nancy was practicing. She thought about the goal she had set for herself, and then suddenly she was not discouraged any more. She *could* learn! She *would* learn!

Back she went to the ice. Over and over she practiced. Sometimes it took her fifteen minutes before she could master the step. Sometimes it took two long hours. But Carol kept at it. And then Coach Brunet smiled.

"*Bien!*" he said. "*Bien!*" That was French for "Good, good."

But one day he did not smile. It was just before a Club competition, and Carol was trying to prepare some new free-skating steps. No matter how hard he tried, Coach Brunet could not get her to keep time with the music.

He threw up his hands in despair and skated over to Carol's mother. "You are wasting your money!"

Nancy helps measure the figures Carol has just cut in the
ice of a midtown New York City rink—all part of learning

he cried. "Your daughter cannot tell one dance step from another."

Mrs. Heiss sat quiet, then she said: "No, I suppose she doesn't know the difference. She has never studied music."

"Then teach her to play the piano," Coach Brunet said firmly.

"Piano lessons on top of skating lessons?" Carol's mother protested. "For three children?" For of course she would not give Carol an advantage the others did not have, too.

Coach Brunet thought hard. He knew that the Heiss family did not have very much money. Suddenly he smiled. He had remembered the name of a friend who once taught piano. "Perhaps she will get your children started," he said. "I will ask her."

Carol's first piano lessons were the gift of this kind teacher. When Carol needed more lessons, she had to have another teacher, and somehow her father managed to stretch the family budget to pay for them. The lessons helped Carol with her skating. She improved every week.

But then one day Coach Brunet skated over to Mrs. Heiss again.

"She must have dancing lessons," he said. "It is important if she is to do her free skating properly."

How could they ever manage? How could they meet the bills? Marie Heiss could only think of one way. She would go to work. But she could not take an office job. She had to be with the children at the rink and with them at home. They were too little to be left alone.

"I will think of something," she told him.

The next day Mrs. Heiss called a number of business offices. At last she found just the job she wanted. It was painting designs for fabrics, and the work could be done at home.

"It is just the thing!" she told her husband. "I can even take my drawing board to the rink and work while I watch over the children."

And that is just what she did. Now she worked while Carol and Nancy cut across the ice and Bruce took his first skating steps. It was clear that all the children loved skating. Carol, in particular, flew as though her skates had wings. The dancing lessons she was taking made her even more graceful.

Skating-club audiences loved to watch her. They cheered ever harder when Nancy joined her sister in in-pairs skating—two skaters doing their figures together. The little girls created a sensation wherever they went. And then a wonderful thing happened. They were able to go to the northern part of Michigan for summer skating.

"We are so lucky," eight-year-old Carol said.

"Lucky," little six-year-old Nancy repeated, bobbing her head. And indeed they were. Very few skaters have a chance to go to rinks that are open all year round.

Carol and Nancy and little Bruce, too, looked forward to their second summer in Michigan. The only sad part was saying goodby to their father. But he would join them soon for his own vacation.

They had not been in Michigan long when Carol became sick with whooping cough. She was very ill, and when Edward Heiss joined his family, he grew so worried about Carol that he rushed her back to New York to the hospital.

She continued to be a very sick little girl. The hospital put her on the danger list. She grew paler and thinner. She weighed only forty-three pounds. But there was a new medicine, and the doctors used it on her. Her life was saved.

For a whole year Carol could not skate. The year passed very slowly for her, and as her health and strength came back, she begged to go to the rink.

"Not yet," her mother said. "Not until the doctors tell us you are strong enough. We must do what they say."

Finally, at the end of a year, they gave permission for Carol to skate again. Would she be able to skate again? Had she forgotten all she had learned?

She laced on her skates. For a moment she stood still at the edge of the rink, and Coach Brunet and her mother watched silently. Then, with a flash of her skates, she skimmed onto the ice. A few graceful turns, a moment of testing herself, and Carol was whirling and leaping across the ice.

"She is better than ever!" Coach Brunet cried.

And she was. She proved this at the most famous ice rink in the world, Madison Square Garden, in New York. She and Nancy were invited to give a pairs exhibition between races at the Silver Skates speed-skating races.

No one had thought of entering them in the races themselves. They were too little. But Nancy and Carol decided that while they were there they would have some fun.

"Let us go in the midget-class speed race—the race for the youngest," Carol said.

Nancy was more than willing. They didn't have speed skates like every one else. They had only their figure skates, but that didn't bother them.

When the time came for the speed race, Carol was ready. She dug in the sharp toe of her skates. The starting gun cracked. Carol took off in a figure skater's flying leap that put her out ahead. She led all the way. No one came close. Ellie Sonneman finished second. Little Nancy came in third. What a surprise for everyone!

Carol never tried speed skating again. She liked the figure skating too much. She wasn't interested in races, but the next year Nancy entered the Silver

Skates again. And this time she won.

Nine days after Carol's tenth birthday, Coach Brunet entered Carol and Nancy in their first important figure-skating competition. They won first place and became the Middle Atlantic Ladies' Pairs champions. The very next day Carol won the Junior Ladies' title.

Was this luck? Neither Coach Brunet nor Marie and Edward Heiss thought so. They entered the girls in a more difficult competition, the Eastern figure-skating at Rye, New York. Ten-year-old Carol won the Eastern Junior Ladies' title. Eight-year-old Nancy, with a front tooth missing, took the Girls' crown.

They had won five silver cups now. And the newspapers were calling them by a new name: "The Golden Kids." Everyone wanted to see them skate. They were invited to appear in ice show after ice show. They were as yet only in grade school, and they were the talk of the skating world.

Marie and Edward Heiss smiled at each other. They had been right. It was not just luck that made the girls champions. They had special talent, and the years of training and hard work were paying off. Anything could lie ahead, even the Olympic championship they had dreamed of.

Ballet classes taught Carol grace of body and sense of musical timing

7

"Education is your life..."

Carol was studying skating hard, but there were her school lessons to study, too, and these could not be neglected.

One day she was working on her history lesson. It was about the American frontier.

"Don't we have frontiers any more?" she asked her mother suddenly.

Her mother nodded. "Everyone has his own frontier," she said. "In the mind. On one side of it, everything is known and tried. On the other side is the part of yourself that has not yet been explored. All of the great adventures in life lie on that other side."

Carol thought. "You mean my own frontiers are the things in skating I haven't learned to do yet?"

"Oh, not just in skating," her mother said. "There is more to life than skating. Exploring your frontiers means finding out what kind of person you can be, too. How much you can learn about all kinds of things. Every school lesson you learn is really exploring. It is finding something new."

Carol's parents never let her neglect her lessons. But it wasn't always easy to keep up in school. Often she had to miss school in order to skate in an important show or competition. And when she was just about to finish sixth grade, the principal of the school demanded a talk with Carol's mother.

"This cannot go on," the principal said. "Carol is out of school too much. She spends so many hours practicing, she does not study her school lessons as much as she should."

"But she is doing all right in school," Carol's mother protested.

"She is not getting as good grades as she could," the principal said. "The time has come for her to choose between school and skating." And the principal did not leave any doubt as to what choice she would make. Skating was all right for fun, but school was far more important for a child's future.

That night Marie and Edward Heiss talked it over. They agreed with the principal that school was more important than anything else. But they knew Carol had a remarkable skating talent, too, and they felt this should not be wasted. Such a God-given talent should be helped, not neglected.

"We can't take skating away from her," Carol's mother said. "It is not something we made her do—it is something she does by choice. Something that is somehow necessary to her. If we take it away from her, Edward, it will leave a hole in her life that books and ideas may not fill."

"Yes," Carol's father said. "We have to find a way so she can have both—without the one interfering with the other."

They studied their problem, and they found an answer. In New York City there is a school called the Professional Children's School. It is attended by children who are in show business. Often, when these children are in a play, they travel around the country performing one week in one city, two weeks in another, a month in another. The Professional Children's School allows them to continue their professional life and at the same time to receive a very fine education.

"The school works very simply," Marie told her husband. "When Carol is home, she will go to morning and afternoon classes. But if she goes away to enter a competition, she takes her lessons along."

"But who corrects them?" Carol's father asked.

"The school does," her mother said. "They give her lesson sheets to take with her and do while she

In 1955 they were both champions—Nancy was the Junior Ladies'

Single champion, Carol, second-ranking Senior Ladies' skater

Carol kept her grades high at Professional Children's School

is away. Every week she has to mail the lessons in, and the teachers correct them."

"What if she is gone when there is an examination?" her father asked.

"They take care of that, too," her mother said. "If Carol is in another city at examination time, she goes to the nearest public school, and a local teacher gives her the test in private. Then the test is sent by that local teacher back to Carol's school. That way, she keeps up with her class, just as if she were in school."

So it was decided that Carol should go to the Professional Children's School. It was expensive. The fee was $600 a year, but both Marie and Edward felt it was worth it.

"We will just work harder," Marie said cheerfully. And that is what they did.

In September, 1953, Carol entered the school. She took English and history and other subjects. Her teachers found her a very good pupil. She did not always get A's, but she was a steady worker. Sometimes her grades dropped when she was away at a skating competition, but then she would work hard to bring them back up. When she was on a trip, she always sent her lessons in by mail.

"The school is good for her in another way," Marie told her husband. "When she wins a competition, the other children do not pay much attention. They are used to people being well known and in the daily newspapers. After all, they all have talents, too. They will be proud of Carol when she wins, but they won't spoil her."

"Good," her father said. "I am glad we could send her to this school. We will send Nancy, too, when the time comes."

And they did. The teachers found that Nancy was quieter and more serious than Carol, just as Coach Brunet had found that Nancy was better at the school figures on the ice.

"Nancy worries more," one teacher said. "She puts more thought into her studies."

Both girls were getting good educations, and that is what their parents wanted. They had never changed their minds about that. And the sisters knew they never would.

Helping younger skaters is all part of the fun of being a champion

8

The accident

In 1950 when Carol and Nancy won their Eastern titles at Rye, New York, a pretty fifteen-year-old girl from Boston, named Tenley Albright, won the Senior Ladies' title. This began two thrilling competitions which were to last for a long time.

The first was the competition between Carol and Tenley, each trying for the highest honors in the skating world.

The second was between Nancy and Carol, and it was different. It had been different since their mother had heard the girls screaming and pulling hair in a fight in their back yard.

Mrs. Heiss ran out and stopped them. "Come into the kitchen," she ordered. The girls obeyed. "Now sit down, both of you," she said, "and listen to me."

The girls sat down. They looked at their mother. Probably she was going to punish them, they thought. But Mrs. Heiss said quietly: "I want you always to remember what I'm going to say to you girls now."

Her voice was so serious that both Carol and Nancy became completely quiet. When their mother was sure she had their full attention, she spoke: "You are growing up now," she said. "And you are going to meet many people. Some of these people you will be able to trust, while there are others you will not. Sometimes you won't be able to tell if people are really your friends or not. But there will always be one person each of you can depend on." She paused for a minute looking at her little daughters. "I mean, you have each other. So I want you to promise me you will never fight and call each other names again. You can compete against each other, but you must stick together."

Nancy stole a look at Carol, and Carol's eyes met hers. They had never really thought before what being sisters meant, but now they saw, and they saw it was something very important.

"I promise, Mama," Carol said.

"I promise, too," Nancy said.

They never forgot that promise. Even when they skated in competition, they were always sisters first

—the Heiss team—and skaters second.

Carol's competition with Tenley Albright developed quickly. Tenley's father was a successful doctor, and he had given her the very best skating instruction. From the first she was a brilliant skater.

When she was eleven, she had had polio. The doctors shook their heads. They were afraid Tenley could never skate again. But Tenley would not give up. She worked and worked. Gradually the effects of the disease went away. In 1949 she became United States Ladies Novice champion. The next year she became the Ladies Junior champion. In 1951 she finished second in the National Ladies' competition, and in 1952 her sparkling free-skating performance in Oslo, Norway, earned her second place in the Winter Olympics.

The year Tenley became National Ladies' champion, Carol became National Junior champion. This meant that in 1953 they would both go to Davos, Switzerland, to represent the United States at the world competition. For the first time they would be skating against each other!

Carol was very excited when she and her mother set off for Switzerland. She knew what a marvelous skater Tenley was, and she was eager to compete against her. Of course she hoped, too, to make a good showing for her country.

No American girl had ever won the world title.

This year Tenley Albright was the favorite. But as the two girls practiced, it was Carol in her gay red and green costume who captured the attention of the crowds gathered in the tiny village high in the Alps mountains. She could not take a turn around the rink without people watching. Still, she was only thirteen, and no one seriously expected her to win although they loved to follow her.

The contest started. There were two days of the school—or compulsory—figures. Tenley was ahead. Then came the day of the finals. It had turned bitter cold. The temperature fell below zero. A shivering wind blew out of the mountains. Two British skaters had to be helped from the ice.

Carol's turn came. Her mother made sure that her white-trimmed red velvet dress was snug and warm. She put her arm around Carol in a quick hug.

"I know it is rough, darling," she said. "And we don't expect you to win the first time. Just do the best you can."

Carol's "best" was something to see. The crowd forgot the cold as they watched her. Carol spun and whirled about the ice. The crowd cheered the entire four minutes she skated.

Then it was Tenley's turn. Of course she was older than Carol and she was a beautiful skater. Her skating began with a flowing, graceful ease, then speeded up as she whirled and leaped. Again she slowed to

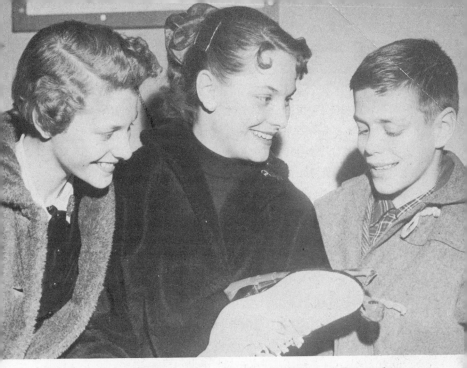

True to their mother's wish, Nancy, Carol, and Bruce have stayed close together, taking pride in what each has done

graceful movements, and then spun into a whirlwind finish that left the crowd out of breath.

"There is no room for improvement," Tenley's coach said. "She is perfect."

The judges agreed. All seven of them voted her first. For the first time an American had won the women's title. Another American, Hayes Alan Jenkins, had won the men's title. And Carol, only thirteen, had finished fourth against the world's best skaters. It was a great day.

Carol came home with two goals in mind. One, to catch up with her school work. Two, to catch up with Tenley!

She had her first chance to try and catch Tenley three weeks later. Both of them appeared at the North American competition in Cleveland. The skaters went through their compulsory figures. Tenley was first. Carol tried hard but placed only fourth.

But there was still the free skating and Carol had made up her mind. Her skating was bold. When the final score was in, Tenley was first. Carol had moved up and was second.

"I will beat her yet!" Carol vowed. But at the national contest at Hershey, Pennsylvania, again it was Tenley first, Carol second.

"Greatest Skating Duel of All Time," the newspapers said.

But Carol was not the only one in the Heiss family who was making news. Nancy had just passed her eighth official Club test, the youngest skater ever to win that medal. She had placed second in the National Novice title contest, too. And nine-year-old Bruce, not to be left out, had won the Eastern Boys' championship. They were truly a skating family.

Every morning the children practiced together. Not a day went by that they did not work with Coach Brunet. But January 1, 1954, was a day that Carol and Nancy will never forget.

The two girls were on the ice together, each doing her own skating. Carol was getting ready for the World Championship competitions to be held the next month in Norway. She was hoping to win.

Marie Heiss sat at the side of the rink with her drawing board on her lap. She was paying little attention to the children. With quick strokes of her pen, she was drawing designs which she hoped to sell to a manufacturer the next day.

Coach Brunet was instructing Carol, and at the same time keeping his eye on Nancy to see how she was doing. The girls were not looking at each other at all. For some reason, as both skated backward, each decided to do a turn. They bumped together. Both of them fell.

It was a stupid accident. The first thing a skater learns is to pay attention to where she is going. Nancy and Carol were both laughing and begging pardons as they got to their feet.

But Carol found she could not stand. Blood was running down her white boot. "You are hurt!" Nancy cried. Coach Brunet came to Carol's side in a spray of ice.

"My skate!" Nancy cried. "I must have cut her!"

"It will be all right," Carol said. "You didn't mean to." And she was carried off the ice.

They rushed Carol to a doctor. He gave her first aid. "Now be sure to keep off your feet," he told her.

For a few days Carol obeyed. But she was thinking about the world competitions. She wanted to be back there practicing.

Family photograph: the Heiss team, Carol, Bruce and Nancy

"My leg feels fine!" she said, hiding her pain. She insisted on getting back to the ice.

But halfway across the rink, her injured leg gave way beneath her. She fell to the ice.

Her father did not care about world titles. Fright and anger shook his voice when Carol got home and he heard what had happened. "You are going to our own doctor," he said. "We're going to find out right now just how bad this is."

He bundled Carol hastily into a taxi. The doctor examined the cut. It was worse than anyone had believed. Nancy's skate had cut nearly to the bone.

The doctor took Carol's father aside. "I must tell you this," he said. "Mr. Heiss, your daughter may never skate again."

Never skate! But her life was skating! That night Carol's father told her mother what the doctor had said to him.

"Oh, Edward!" Marie cried. "It will break her heart if it is true!"

Edward nodded. "I think," he said slowly, "that we must tell her how serious the injury is. But I do not think we need to tell her the doctor said she may never skate again. Instead, I think we must encourage her. Perhaps it will help."

The next morning they talked to Carol. They told her how the skate had injured her, how the muscle had been damaged. "Now then," her mother said, "you will just have to work at it. That is the way to face trouble like this."

And fourteen-year-old Carol did work. She knew that if she didn't, she might be crippled forever. She remembered how Tenley had been sick with polio, but now her rival was skating and winning. "I can, too!" Carol declared.

She had to go to the doctor's office for treatment. Carol never skipped one. Whenever her mother asked: "Do you want to do the dusting for me?" or her father said: "Want to walk along to the store with me?" Carol suffered the pain and went along. Exercise was very important.

But though Carol suffered pain, little Nancy was suffering in even a worse way.

"I am to blame!" she cried. "It was all my fault."

"It wasn't either," Carol said. "It was an accident. I am to blame as much as you are. I wasn't looking where I was going. Why, it might have happened to you."

But poor Nancy was unhappy. She was going to the rink alone now, as Mrs. Heiss was staying home with Carol, and she did not seem to want to go.

"You must not blame yourself this way," her mother said. "Carol is right—it was an accident. Run along now, and have a good practice."

With dragging feet Nancy set out. Every day her eyes seemed to get more unhappy. And then one day when she came home, she stumbled into the room she shared with Carol and flung herself down on the bed, sobbing her heart out.

Carol limped quickly to her. "Nancy, what is the matter?" she begged. "Tell me, what is it?"

"I am not going to skate any more," she wept. "Not ever again."

"But you can't quit!" Carol cried. "Nancy, you are a wonderful skater. You must not say that."

"I won't go back there!" Nancy sobbed. "They—they think I did it on purpose."

Carol stared at her. "Did it on purpose!" she exclaimed. "Who thinks that? Who said such an awful, hurtful thing?"

"They all do," Nancy wept. "They all whisper

together. They say I was jealous. They say I hurt you on purpose so you couldn't beat me. When I skate by, the kids yell: 'There goes Killer Heiss!' "

Carol's face went white. What a terrible thing! She dropped down beside Nancy, putting her arms around her. "They are the ones that are jealous—of both of us!" she said fiercely. "We will show them, Nancy! I am going to skate in the Nationals in March if I have to do it on one foot! Tomorrow morning I am going to get started. When they see us skating together again, they will know how unfair they have been, what lies they have been telling, and they will not talk any more."

The Nationals were only two months away. Carol's injured leg made it much more difficult to skate, but she started again, gritted her teeth, and kept at it.

Nancy helped all she could. And when the competitions came, Carol skated. Injury or no injury, she did a brilliant job. Then Tenley skated, and excitement ran through the crowd. Which girl would the judges pick? They were both so good.

Once more it was Tenley first and Carol second.

"Maybe I didn't win the competition," Carol told Nancy when they got home. "But you and I won something else. We showed everyone who whispered about you just how wrong they were."

She was right. The sharp tongues were silenced for good and all.

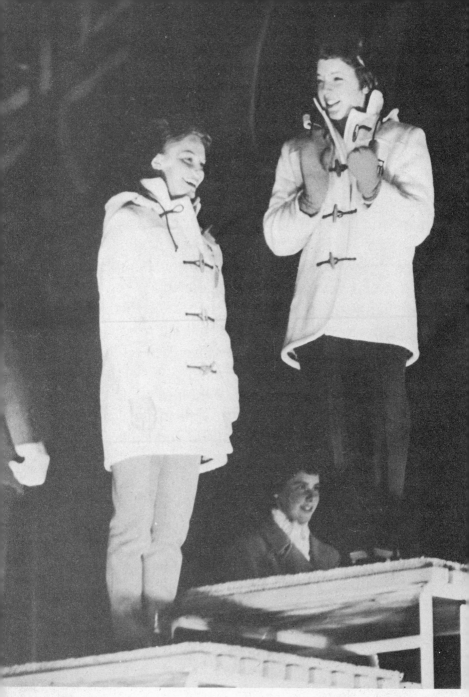

Would Carol ever be anything but the runner-up to Tenley Albright?

9

Tragedy and triumph

Carol was still worried about her injured leg, and she didn't think twice when her mother suggested that she look up some information about cancer, the dread disease that causes strange growths of cells in the body. Her mother was always thinking up projects: It was one way she could help Carol learn.

She did the work, wondering a little why her mother had picked this subject. Then one day her mother said: "In September, I am going to have an operation."

Carol's eyes opened wide. "An operation?" she said. "Mama, what for?"

"Oh, nothing very important," her mother said. But slowly the truth came to Carol. Now she knew why her mother had asked her to study. It had been her way of preparing Carol for some terrible news.

"Mama, tell me. Is the operation for cancer?"

"Yes, Carol," her mother said quietly, and a little shiver ran through Carol. She was frightened. She caught at her mother's hand.

"Does it mean you will die, Mama?" she asked.

"Many people have successful cancer operations," her mother said. "You know who Babe Didrikson Zaharias is, don't you?"

"The great woman golfer?" Carol answered.

"Well, didn't you know she had an operation for cancer? The same one I am going to have. And she is back playing golf now."

"But, Mama—," Carol said.

"No *buts* now," her mother said. "We are going to have no long faces just because there may be trouble. That is not the way we meet things, is it?"

Carol tried to be cheerful for her mother's sake. Marie Heiss went to the hospital as planned. The operation was performed. In a very short time she was allowed to get up, and every day she went up and down the halls to visit other patients and to joke with the nurses and doctors.

"I always know where to find you when I come to visit," Carol said. "I just listen to hear which room the laughter is coming from."

Before too long her mother was home. She was

just as cheerful and jolly as she had been in the hospital, but Carol was not fooled. Sometimes she saw flashes of pain come to her mother's face, sometimes a shadow in her eyes. One day when her father was working in the garden, Carol went out to him.

"Daddy," she said, "Mama isn't as well as she is pretending to be, is she?"

Her father put down his tools. He turned to his daughter. "No, Carol," he said, "she isn't."

Carol's heart sank. Her eyes searched her father's face. "Does it mean—?" she whispered.

Her father nodded, pain in his own eyes. "I am afraid so," he said. "We must be prepared, Carol."

The day came for Carol to set off for Vienna where the world competition would be held. "I don't think your mother should go with you," her father said. "I think the trip might be too much for her."

Much as she would miss her mother, Carol agreed. But Marie Heiss would not listen. "I am going," she said. Because they both knew how much it meant to her, neither Carol nor her father tried to argue.

Carol and her mother got on the plane. Mrs. Heiss was in great pain, though. She tried not to show it. The trip was hard for her, and Carol's heart was torn with grief for her mother.

But when they reached Vienna, Mrs. Heiss went to the rink for every practice period, every competition. She hid the pain from everyone.

Carol tried to match her mother's great courage. At every practice lesson she tried to improve. She hoped so much that she would win that year, for her mother's sake.

Tenley Albright was working hard, too. The year before, when Carol had had to stay home because of her injured leg, Tenley had taken a bad fall on poor ice, and had lost her title. Now she was determined to get it back.

The competition began. First, the skating figures. Carol was very worried about her mother, and in spite of herself, the worry affected her performance. When the first four figures were completed, she was way back in sixth place.

The free skating came. Tenley had prepared a wonderful exhibition, full of new leaps. They were called a "stage loop jump" and "three's in spirals into a camel hump." They were very difficult, and Tenley did them brilliantly. The crowd cheered. The judges gave her several 5.9 scores—a six is perfect.

Then Carol put on a performance that had the crowd screaming. Since her accident she had had to learn to jump from either foot, and her skating was thrilling to see.

But it was Tenley who won again, Carol who came in second. Tenley had her world title. And Carol held out her hand though she had wanted the title very badly herself.

"You were wonderful," she told Tenley.

"It is the biggest thrill of my life," Tenley confessed. "Losing something makes you appreciate it all the more."

Now Carol had just one goal. She must win a first over Tenley. For her mother. Never had she worked so hard. Yet, in both the Nationals and the North American champion contests later that winter, she came in second.

"I have to do better!" she cried. "I have to win."

"You are only fifteen," Coach Brunet said. "Tenley is nearly twenty."

Carol would not accept this as an excuse. She knew that Tenley had received a number of professional offers, and she was glad Tenley turned them down in order to finish college and to become a doctor like her father. Now Carol could catch up with her before Tenley retired. And before the dreaded cancer might take her mother from her.

In April, 1955, Marie Heiss went back to the hospital. Again she came home from the operation, but she was thinner now. The lines of pain showed.

The Winter Olympics would be held in Cortina, Italy, in January 1956. Carol was chosen for the team—the youngest girl ever to skate for the United States in the Olympics. If only she could win the gold medal! It might be the last chance she would have to win a first over Tenley for her mother.

January came. Marie Heiss calmly announced that she was going to Italy with Carol and Coach Brunet. Edward remembered how his wife had suffered the year before in Vienna. He knew that she needed long, hot baths to ease her pain, and in the hotel where the American team would stay it might not be possible for her to have a private bath.

"I will only let you go if you take a room with a private bath," he said. "You can get a doctor's order so they will know how important it is, and give you the room."

Marie shook her head. "I don't want to make a fuss," she said. "I won't take a doctor's order. Carol and I will find a room outside the team quarters. No one must know that I am sick."

And no one did know. No one suspected the real reason why Carol and her mother searched for rooms with a private bath on their arrival at Cortina. All the other Americans were staying together. Gossip began. The whispered word went around that the Heisses felt too important to stay with the others.

In a newspaper Carol read that she thought she was "too good" to share the American team's hotel. It upset her terribly.

"Mama," she begged. "Let me tell them the truth. We don't think we are too good. It is just because you are so ill."

But her mother wouldn't let her tell. She did not

At last! In the world championship competition of 1956, Carol was first, with Tenley second, and Ingrid Wendl of Austria, the third

want pity for Carol, and she did not want it for herself either.

The bad feeling cleared away briefly on January 20 when the American team celebrated Carol's sixteenth birthday. There was a beautiful cake, and everyone sang "Happy Birthday."

But this was a special birthday for another reason. It marked the end of the ten years that the Brunets had said Carol would need to become the champion.

"Remember, Mother?" Carol said when they got back to their rooms. "I am right on time."

"I have a feeling this is the year," her mother said. Silently Carol promised herself that she would give this final gift to her mother.

The next day they went shopping to get some warmer clothes as it had turned very cold. They met Tenley Albright in the store, and they all had hot chocolate together. Tenley had hurt her leg in practice, and Carol asked her about it.

"I think it is better," Tenley said. "Father is flying over. He will fix it."

Back in New York, sports writers weren't interested in shopping trips or hot chocolate. "Carol Heiss and her mother are not popular with the American team," they wrote. "They act like 'big shots.'" Every paper Mr. Heiss picked up seemed to carry the same stories. Worried, Edward Heiss wrote to his wife and daughter to see what was the matter. And then finally the day of the long-awaited contest arrived.

Tenley knew as well as Carol that no American woman had ever won the skating gold medal at the Olympics. She was going to try as hard as Carol. "I am going to skate until I fall apart," she declared.

The school figures came first. Carol had never done so well. She finished nearly even with Tenley. The crowd was excited. They enjoyed the competition between the two skaters. It made a thrilling afternoon of wonderful skating. The big question was whether or not the older, almost perfect champion from Boston could beat the latest challenge of the exciting blonde Carol.

In the free skating Tenley skated first. It was a wonderful performance. When she came off the ice, she was completely tired out. "My ankle hurts like anything," she confessed. "But I knew I could stand it for four minutes." And the judges and sports writers agreed it had been worth it. Her performance had been nearly perfect.

Could Carol beat her? It was an hour later when her turn came. Late afternoon darkness had settled in. The bright lights cut through it. There was a heavy wind. It was freezing cold.

The crowd cheered as Carol skated onto the ice. But to her there was only one person in the stands: her mother. Carol skated for her.

Those four minutes were called "the most daring

After her 1956 victory, Carol was the center of interest of photographers and public at the little Austrian sports center

program ever skated by a woman at the Olympics." But when they were over and Carol tried to smile for the cameras all she knew was that she was exhausted and nearly frozen.

"Get to your room quickly and change," Coach Brunet ordered her.

She didn't even wait to see if she had won. Her mother hurried to the room, too, and she and Coach Brunet began to rub Carol's fingers to warm them. Out on the rink the score was announced. Tenley was still the champion. Carol still was second.

A newspaper man pounded on the door. Brunet opened it. "Get Carol out here," the newsman said. "We want a picture of her kissing Tenley."

"Are you crazy?" Brunet asked. "Get it tomorrow when they get their medals. This girl is exhausted and half frozen." He was sure the writer understood.

But the man insisted.

Coach Brunet shut the door.

The next morning that shut door was known around the world. All the papers wrote how "stuck up" Carol Heiss was. It didn't do a bit of good when Carol and Tenley had their pictures taken together for an hour the next day. It didn't even do any good when, in a radio interview, she praised Tenley. The papers called her a bad sport.

It hurt Carol. And losing the gold medal she had wanted so much to win before her mother's death hurt, too. But now she saw another chance to make her mother happy.

In two weeks the world champion competition would be held in Germany. Tenley would be there. Carol would be there, too. This time, could Carol come in first?

It was twenty degrees below zero when the Heisses arrived in Garmisch. In vain they searched for hotel rooms. They could find nothing. It seemed like a miracle when the Canadian team checked in and its manager offered Carol and her mother rooms with private baths. With deep gratitude they accepted.

Two days later the manager of the American team ordered them to change hotels. He wanted all the Americans quartered together. Of course he did not know about Mrs. Heiss' sickness, and he was not at all pleased when she did not want to move.

"We are comfortable here," she said. "We would rather stay where we are."

She was paying for the rooms herself, so the manager couldn't make them move, but he did not like it. And the next day the papers came out with bigger stories: "Officials Blast Carol Heiss." Some said that Carol and Tenley were jealous of each other.

I must win, Carol told herself fiercely. Already her mother was so ill that she remained in her room during some of the events. But she was there for the skating and when the first school figures ended with Tenley slightly ahead, she comforted Carol.

"It isn't over yet," she said. "You still have a chance."

By a tremendous effort, Carol finished the school figures with a slight lead. It was the first time she had ever been ahead of Tenley!

Now came the finals. The crowds saw skating that they would remember all their lives. Tenley skated first, and every ounce of skill and grace she had went into her performance. When she came off the ice, she shook her head. "If that doesn't do it," she said, "I can't do it."

Snow was falling as Carol skated out onto the rink. In the stands her mother and her father's parents, who had come from Munich to watch, sat almost holding their breath. The music Carol had chosen to skate to was "If I Were King," and Carol turned it into music for a queen. For four minutes her leaps and spins sent her pony tail cutting the air like a whip. She was marvelous! When she stopped in a shower of ice, the crowd leaped to its feet, cheering. One judge forgot himself and clapped, though judges are not supposed to.

"Six! Six! Six!" the crowd shouted, demanding a perfect score.

Had she done it? Carol did not know. She waited, not saying a word. Beside her, her mother and grand-parents were also silent.

One by one the scores were announced. There were nine judges, and each time Carol's performance was given the same score—5.9. No judge differed. She was judged as nearly perfect as it was possible to be. She had won! *She* was the world-champion woman figure skater.

"Mother, I did it! I did it!" Carol cried. Tears she had never shed in defeat poured down her face now.

Never had she known such excitement. Her mother kissed her. Her grandparents kissed her. Coach Brunet kissed her. Everyone was laughing and crying at once. What a wonderful moment! The years of work, the years of giving up everything else to reach a goal, the sacrifices her parents had made were flooding back in rich rewards. Carol could see how hard work pays off. In her mother's eyes she saw happiness, and in her daddy's telegram of love she saw his pride in her, and his trust. It was a beautiful, wonderful moment.

But it was more than that. For victory brings more than happiness. And it was Pierre Brunet who helped Carol see this. When the cheers and the excitement had died down a little, Coach Brunet led Carol apart from the others. He looked down at her medal, and he said:

"Yes, it is beautiful. But soon you will put it in a drawer to collect dust. Where, then, will you find the real values of what you have done today?"

Carol looked at him and Pierre's look met hers.

"Coming in first is not that important, Carol," he said. "Unless in it you have found one thing."

"What is that?" Carol asked him.

"Your hidden strength," he said. "The strength to know what is in you. How much you can do. How far you can reach—if you are willing to try."

For the battle is never over. There are always new things to do. Once her mother had said there were new frontiers she could conquer—frontiers of learning and discovering. Frontiers which she, herself, could open. And now Coach Brunet, in the moment of her first victory over a wonderful skater, was telling her the same thing.

Carol thought to herself: "How lucky I have been. I have parents who have understood that we must always go forward. A coach who has helped me! I will not fail them. And I will not fail myself, either."

Carol was invited to go to Berlin to skate. It was a great honor, and she and her mother made the trip. Carol skated beautifully, thrilling all those who watched her. But in Berlin her mother grew very sick. The pain was too great. Her courage was pushed beyond its limits.

Carol and her mother left for home immediately. There were many great things planned for Carol when she arrived and Mrs. Heiss would not let her skip one of them. The Mayor of New York gave her an official greeting. Canada invited her to come and skate. There were parades and cheering crowds.

But Carol's smile was sad. Her mother had to stay at home. Carol carried on, for she had learned that part of success is carrying the burdens you have so well that others do not see them.

Two weeks after her return home, Carol met Tenley in the Nationals. It was their last competition of 1956. Each of them had won a previous meet. This would be a final test.

But there was something more important than the skating between them and each of them knew it. Newspapers had written of the jealousy between them. As they laced on their skates, Tenley spoke:

"I don't like these stories, Carol. I don't like people saying we are enemies."

In Carol's home, Ozone Park, Long Island, a special cabinet was built to hold the trophies of her important victories

"I don't either," Carol answered.

"We have to face it," Tenley said, and the two girls talked it over. They decided that if they should read something bad about the other, each would know it was not true.

"We know each other," Tenley said, looking straight into Carol's eyes.

"So we know what is true," Carol said, "and we will always be good friends."

"Right," Tenley said. Then she grinned. "But that doesn't mean I won't try to beat you."

In these Nationals it was again Tenley's turn to win. The judges rated her first and Carol second. When the two girls shook hands after the competition, their eyes met. And in each other's eyes they read the same thing: "Friends, still."

Summer came, and though Marie Heiss was very

ill, she and the children went to Michigan for the skating season there. Marie Heiss knew she had not long to live, but she had made up her mind to live fully all the time she had left. It was what she wanted.

Carol practiced that summer harder than ever. She knew Tenley was doing the same thing, and she knew that next year's competition would be the most demanding of her career. Her mother encouraged her constantly. But that summer she could not go on. Carol was the oldest, and it fell to her to take charge. She grew up in those days. She made the arrangements. They flew their mother back to New York. Once there, Marie refused to go to a hospital.

"I want to be in my own home with my family around me," she said.

"Then it shall be that way," Carol's father replied.

And so it was. Every night after work Edward hurried home, grief and love for his wife showing in his eyes. During the day, the children were near their mother. They did all the work and whenever there was time, they came to her with stories to cheer her. To their mother's room they took the gift of laughter. They were making her last days happy, as she had helped fill their lives with joy.

On October 30, 1956, their mother died. Now the papers learned suddenly why Carol and her mother had had their hotel rooms apart from the others. They were ashamed of the things they had said because they knew Carol had not been a bad sport at all but had only loved her mother.

The Heiss family had been prepared for Marie's death. They knew that it must come and they believed that death is not a frightening end to this life but a beautiful beginning of eternal life. Their love went with their mother, and they were glad for her that she had gone to a place where no more pain could reach her.

Yet the house in Ozone Park seemed empty without their mother. She had been so great a part of their courage, so central a part of their lives, they could not help but feel lost now that she had left them.

"I don't know how I will carry on without her," their father said, "but I will do the best I can."

The children clustered around him, giving him their love, taking support from him, and giving it to him. Marie would not want them to break down. All her life she had had courage, and now she would want them to have it, too. She would want them to go on.

They did. Carol spent long hours at the ice rink, not forgetting her mother but not letting grief destroy her. Bruce and Nancy did, too. And their father straightened his shoulders and carried on. They were honoring Marie. Each in his own way saying: You gave me so much. I won't fail you now.

Tenley was practicing for the next meet, too—six hours a day in Boston. But there were many things in

Tenley's mind besides skating, many decisions about things other than sports that she must make.

Then on January 20, 1957, Carol's seventeenth birthday, Tenley Albright sent a telegram to the United States Figure Skating Association. *She was withdrawing from all future contests!*

Tenley had made her decision after much thought. She had made a fine record at Radcliffe College. She had made such good grades that Harvard Medical School was accepting her as a student after only three years instead of the usual four. And Tenley had always wanted to be a doctor.

"Well," Bruce said, "there goes your contest."

Carol did not smile. Never again would she be able to compete against Tenley. For so many years she had been trying to find out who was the better skater— Tenley or she. She had looked forward to the next meet, the next time she might have a chance to skate better, setting skating standards at an all time high. And she knew that skating against Tenley had brought out the best in her. Now it would be up to her alone.

"I am going to miss Tenley," she said.

Her father understood her disappointment. Yet in his wisdom he knew that some day Carol would understand Tenley's decision. If the time came, he hoped that Carol would make the same kind of decision herself.

By 1959, Carol had been Women's World Figure Skating Champion three years

10

More glory

In 1957 Carol graduated from the Professional Children's School. Many colleges throughout the country offered to give her scholarships. That would mean that she would not have to pay for her education. Scholarships are sometimes offered to those who are very good at basketball or football. Such students, in whatever line, bring fame to the school. Of course, in Carol's case the fame would be in skating.

Carol considered all the offers. Finally she decided to accept the scholarship from New York University. She chose this school because it was near home.

Carol had many duties now. She was trying to run the home, to manage the meals and the cooking and cleaning now that her mother was gone. She was the oldest and she felt this was her responsibility. Her father helped as much as he could, often doing the cooking. Nancy and Bruce both took on their share of work around the house.

Her skating career prevented her from taking a full load of subjects at college, so a special program was arranged for her. She took two or three subjects each term instead of the usual five and all her classes were in the afternoon so that her mornings were free for practice. To catch up, she would go to summer school for she did not want to get behind in her studies.

In skating Carol had one goal now: She wanted to win the Olympic gold medal in 1960. She began to get ready, though the Games were still three years off.

The first step came at Rochester, New York. She wore a bright red costume, and a shining crown. At the end of the first day Carol was far ahead of all the other skaters.

It was exciting, too, because in the stands, cheering for her were the men's champion David Jenkins and his older brother, Hayes Alan Jenkins, who had been world champion for four years before retiring. Carol's heart beat a little faster when she saw Hayes. She liked him very much.

But there was not too much time to think about Hayes or anything else. That same month she had to journey to Colorado Springs to defend her world figure-skating crown. It would be a hard test.

Two Austrian skaters, Ingrid Wendl and Hanna Walter, were runners-up to Carol in world's figure-skating championship

The contest was held at the Broadmoor Ice Palace. Over 3,000 fans were there to see her. The music for her performance began. Carol came onto the ice. She began a spin. *And she slipped!*

A gasp went up from the crowd. Would it count against her? Would the judges mark her down because of that slip? Carol recovered herself quickly and did some daring leaps and double figures. When it was over the judges decided that her slip at the start had not been serious. They gave her a high rating. Carol kept her crown.

She went on, the next month, to win the United States title. Now she had three crowns—the world,

High in the Alps, champion practices free skating technique that was going to win her the 1960 Winter Olympics medal

North America and the United States titles. Could she keep it up until 1960?

Two of her titles were at stake in 1958—world champion and United States champion. The world competition was held in Paris, and imagine what happened! *Carol slept late!* It had never happened before. But sure enough, the morning of the competition, she didn't hear her alarm. On and on she slept. Suddenly something brought her wide awake. She caught up her clock and looked at it. It couldn't be true! It couldn't be this late!

She jumped from bed and pulled on her clothes. She dashed from the hotel and out to the rink. She barely had time to get into her costume, to lace on her skates when it was her turn.

Feeling shaky, she went out onto the ice. Once more she made a poor start, and the great crowd groaned in disappointment. Quickly Carol pulled herself together. She would just have to skate better and make up for that bad start.

How she skated! No one had ever seen such a display. The crowds cheered and cheered. People were shouting and jumping up and down. For the first time in history, three judges gave Carol perfect 6 totals. No one had ever before received more than *one* 6 in world-champion competition.

David Jenkins won the men's world championship. All America was happy for them. Then, in March, they both added to their honors by winning the United States titles at Minneapolis.

Now Carol had a chance to win three crowns again. The year was 1959—the year before the Olympics. Could she do it? The first test came at the national competitions, and this was a great day for the Heiss family. Carol won first place. But the thing that made her happiest was that Nancy was right behind her as second-place winner.

"Wonderful!" Carol cried, hugging her sister tight. "You are just wonderful!"

A week later Carol captured her second 1959 crown at the North American contests in Toronto, Canada. How she skated that day! She used a very brilliant figure in skating called a "double-axel Paulsen," and she coupled it with many other difficult figures. There was no question who the winner was when the contest was over.

Now came the third try. The scene was Colorado Springs again. And once more she got off to a terrible start! Nothing would go right. At the end of the first part of the championship test, her score was worse than it had been in years—it was below five.

The crowd groaned. Their favorite would never make it. Then the groans turned to cheers. Carol was fighting back. Her silver skates traced poetry on the ice. No one had ever skated like this! It was marvelous. Wonderful!

Carol finished with the biggest margin in totals of her career. Though she had made a bad start, she had not let it defeat her. She had just fought harder, and the crown was hers. The European champion came in second. Nancy Heiss made the proud showing of placing eighth, which was very good in world competition.

By the end of 1959 Carol had won four straight world titles, three straight national titles, and two straight North American titles. She was the most popular skater the world had known for years. There was only one title she had not won—the Olympic championship. You might think that with all her victories Carol would have been sure of it.

"It is harder now," she said. "It is harder to stay on top than to get there. People wish you luck—but now you are more alone."

Carol was alone because every champion is alone. It is natural that everyone wants to defeat the champion. One thing more exciting than a great champion is a *new* champion, and now fans were cheering for other skaters rather than Carol. Carol's skating was always exciting, but crowds expected that of her now. They demanded it! And with the pride of a champion, she could not disappoint them. Each time she stepped out onto the ice, she had to do better. Like a true champion, she was competing against herself.

Early in 1960, Carol went to Seattle to the national championships. She knew that the first three winners would be picked to represent the United States in the Olympic Games. And more than anything, Carol wanted that Olympic gold medal. It was the one medal she had promised her mother.

Carol won. She was first on the cards of all the judges. Inside she felt happy. She knew she was ready for the Olympics.

Carol was first woman athlete to take the Olympic oath for all competitor

11

The great test

Now began the last preparation. Perhaps you would think that with so many years of training and work behind her, Carol would have nothing to do but wait for the great day.

That is far from the truth. This last year, Carol must work harder than ever. The greatest skaters from all over the world would be at the Olympics. Carol would have to skate her very best to win and she would not be able to skate her best without every-day hours of practice.

Once a newspaper called her both "Princess and Slave." That surely seemed to be true. She was a princess beloved by cheering crowds, greeted by mayors, swept along in parades. But she was a slave, too.

Every day she was up at 5:30 in the morning. By seven she and Nancy and Bruce were at the rink, reporting to Coach Brunet after the long ride to the city. For five hours Carol practiced under the sharp eyes of her coach.

Then she rushed to her classes at New York University. They lasted until four. After that she hurried home, helped with the work of the house and did her home work. At nine o'clock sharp she had to be in bed. There wasn't a day that was very different.

If she won a competition, if her picture was in the paper, she had no chance to get spoiled. At home Nancy and Bruce played tricks on her, called her "the old lady" to tease her. Her father said she was his right hand.

A neighbor helped the Heiss family keep up their seven-room house, but there was plenty for Carol to do. She was a good cook—southern fried chicken was her favorite. Sometimes her father took over the cooking when he came from the bakery. He didn't want Carol to get too tired.

The summer before the Olympics, Carol went with Bruce, Nancy and her father to a cabin they owned in the north woods. There skating was forgotten for a few brief weeks.

They had a wonderful time. There were all kinds of things to do—swimming and fencing and water skiing. Happy meals, sometimes picnic style. And wonderful days. They were over too soon. Now came the great test—the 1960 Winter Olympics, held in Squaw Valley, California. It is a beautiful valley, nine thousand feet high in the heart of the Sierra Nevada mountains. White walls of snow cut it off completely from the outside world. The nearest city is Reno, Nevada, forty miles away.

Ten years ago the valley lay still and silent, known only by the planes which flew overhead under the blue roof of the sky and by the animals whose tracks cut the snow. Today an eight-lane highway carries winter-sports lovers there into a playland of ski lifts and ski runs. A covered ice rink seats 9,000 people. There are fine practice rinks. A huge restaurant serves meals. There are small communities of houses and hotels for visitors. Ten million dollars were spent to change the winter wilderness into this winter-sports center and it was all built for the 1960 Olympic Winter Games.

Carol arrived at Squaw Valley with Coach Pierre Brunet. There were thousands of skaters and skiers from more than thirty countries. Twenty-six girls from thirteen nations were entered in the women's figure-skating competition. All wanted to win.

One skater whom Carol had counted on was not there—her sister Nancy. They had hoped they could both compete, and had hoped to finish first and second. But the dream had vanished a few weeks earlier

The judges at the Olympics watch closely as Carol whirls

to a close of her free-skating series of leaps and turns

Returning the verdict that spelled victory for Carol, the judges of this figure-skating event hold their scores high

when Nancy twisted her ankle. She could not skate for the whole winter.

Alone, Carol knew this would be her last chance to win the gold medal she had promised her mother. She had promised herself that she would retire from competition after the Games. She wanted to marry and have a family. There were some reports going around that a certain young man had won her heart.

Carol was a favorite at Squaw Valley. She delighted the skaters and skiers from every country. One Soviet newsman sent a report back to his newspaper in Moscow, telling about the wonderful friendship found in Squaw Valley. He told how Carol and the Russian Olympic speed-skating girl champion were seen playing with the wooden dolls the Russians had brought to Squaw Valley.

"How do you like Carol Heiss?" reporters asked the Russian girl.

"I like her very much," she said. "As a friend I love her. Doesn't everyone?"

Carol's warm, easy personality helped her as the figure-skating competition began. It was to last for four days and it was terribly tiring for all the skaters.

But Carol would not let herself become nervous. As the competition began, she moved along the benches talking to rival skaters, laughing and joking with them. Sixteen skaters went on before Carol every day. That was a long, hard wait, and Coach

Carol shows the Olympic Gold Medal that crowned her years of winning national and world figure-skating championships

There is no greater thrill than a parade up Broadway in New York City. Carol was welcomed home by such a celebration

Brunet paced up and down, puffing on a huge black cigar to calm him. When Carol's turn came, he stared with expert eyes at her lone figure as she whirled about the ice in her brilliant red costume.

She wore a small crown on her hair, and each day Coach Brunet had to admit that she skated like a queen. Each day when the judges held up her score Carol's lead over her rivals increased.

The fourth day came. This was the day of the free-skating event which counts for 40% of each skater's total score. This was the event in which Carol was at her best.

She had prepared the most difficult program she could think of because this time she was skating to win in memory of her mother. She included 20 of the 26 difficult jumps that are possible in free-skating. The most difficult was called the "left-and-right double axel." The powerful skater Dick Button had introduced it when he was Olympic champion. To do it, a skater takes off in a spinning jump first from one foot, then the other, in quick succession. Carol was the only girl to do it.

The crowds cheered and cheered again when her performance ended. Then they fell silent. What would the score be?

A gasp went up when the Japanese judge held up marks of 5.5 for general impression and 5.6 for merit. These were poor marks. Then they remembered that he had graded everyone lower than the other judges. Two other judges gave her 5.9, three gave her 5.8. She had won her gold medal!

The tears in her eyes as she accepted it, the little prayer in her heart to her mother, showed how much this meant to her.

After the many pictures were taken, Carol whispered: "I wish Mother could have been here today to share this. And Daddy, too."

Now writers from the newspapers flocked around. They threw questions at her. What were her future plans? Would she turn professional? Would she agree to perform in the Ice Follies?

Carol looked to Coach Brunet for help but she was the one who had to answer these questions. "I have won every prize I ever hoped for," she said finally. "I may compete next year. Right now I am not interested in turning professional. I have a year and a half to go in school, and I would like to finish. I would like to learn French and German so I can understand what they are saying when I don't do a perfect delayed axel."

Back in New York, Papa Heiss agreed with his daughter. "She is old enough to decide for herself," he told writers who called on him.

The sports writers weren't satisfied. Some guessed that she could earn $100,000 a year if she turned professional. They thought she deserved it after the long years of discipline and family sacrifice.

But Carol went on to Canada where she won her fifth world title. Again the sports writers clustered around her. This was the last competition of 1960. What were her plans?

Carol stared directly back into their eyes. With the firmest manner a 20-year-old girl can show when she is five-feet-three inches tall and weighs 107 pounds, she said: "I don't know what I am going to do next year."

But even as she spoke there were stories going around that Carol had plans she had not mentioned.

Carol and Hayes Alan Jenkins were married in late April of 1960

12

Carol today

Four weeks after her Olympic triumph Carol invited the newspaper writers to see her. Hayes Alan Jenkins was with her. The reporters thought they knew what her news was. They had heard talk about her.

Carol smiled and joked with the writers, most of whom she knew. Then she told them:

"I am going to marry Hayes Alan Jenkins." The newsmen cheered and shook hands with Hayes. This was a wonderful match. Hayes was the 1956 Olympic skating champion and four times the world champion. The two made a handsome couple. Hayes was slender. At twenty-seven he had a lean, strong figure. He smiled down at his pretty bride-to-be.

No one was really surprised. They had noticed

Hayes and Carol together. Recently he had been graduated from Harvard Law School and he had a good future to look forward to.

Carol and Hayes had known each other for a long time. They had first met at the Brunets', and had skated in pairs competition together. As Carol was winning her victories, Hayes' brother, David, had been winning in the men's division, and Hayes had always been there to cheer him on—and to cheer Carol, too.

Carol and Hayes had come to love each other. That was the most important thing. They knew their life ahead lay together.

Then at the news conference Carol said something else—and this was more surprising than news of her coming marriage.

"In the past," she began, "I have said I would not turn professional. I had to say that—and mean it— or I would have lost my amateur standing in the skating associations."

The writers leaned forward. They knew this was true. "Now things have changed," Carol said. "I no longer insist that I will not skate as a professional."

Newsmen rushed for the telephones. This was big news. *Carol Heiss was turning professional.*

She had received many offers. Movie makers wanted her. TV shows and ice shows were seeking her. Carol felt she could no longer turn her back.

For fifteen years her family had sacrificed so that she might have the training and opportunities she needed. It had cost a great deal. One pair of skates cost $150. Costumes often cost $100 or more. Trips and lessons were expensive. Carol thought now of the careers of Nancy and Bruce. They still had much training, much expense ahead of them, and though her father never complained, she knew what a heavy burden he had carried.

She wanted to help. In just one year she could earn a great deal of money. She could help Nancy and Bruce. She could save money for things she and Hayes would want. So she had decided both to get married and to skate as a professional.

On April 30, 1960, Carol Elizabeth Heiss stood in the entrance of St. Thomas Episcopal Church on New York's Fifth Avenue. She wore a lovely white gown with a full skirt and a touch of lace at the throat. Like all Carol's dresses, it was simply designed but it was the most beautiful she would wear in her life.

Her hand closed tightly on her father's arm. He smiled at her, pride and love in his eyes. In the church, the organ began to play, and Carol's father led her slowly into the church.

The wedding guests stood, paying her tribute as she came down the aisle. Her hands held a white prayer book with a spray of white flowers on it. Pearls glowed softly around her neck.

The marriage joined two great Olympic skaters. Carol made

Hayes joined her at the altar, a flower that matched those she carried pinned to his coat. His eyes lit up as he looked at Carol.

Together they faced the altar. The Reverend Frederick M. Morris began the solemn words of the ceremony. Beside her, her sister Nancy, who was her maid of honor, held back sudden tears.

When the ceremony was over, Carol slipped her hand under Hayes' arm and walked back down the church aisle—Carol Elizabeth Jenkins now. Mrs. Hayes Jenkins—a bride.

As they stepped out onto the church steps, the sun

an unusually pretty and happy bride for the picture takers

flooded down on them, and from the street where hundreds of their fans were jammed waiting for this moment, a great cheer rose. Hayes and Carol waved. Picture after picture was taken. Carol knew it was the most wonderful moment of her life.

There was a wedding party afterwards at the home of friends, and the most beautiful wedding cake she had ever seen. It was topped with wedding bells that seemed almost to ring out. And the most beautiful thing about the cake was that her father had baked it. With a cry of happiness, she threw her arms around him and hugged him tight.

There's nothing like running your own home to find happiness. Now Carol is not only a housewife but is also a movie star

Then Carol and Hayes slipped away. A shower of rice followed them. The wedding trip was happiness from start to finish and when it was over Carol and Hayes settled in Ohio. There he entered an important law firm.

Carol loved her new home. She loved keeping house and cooking for Hayes. Every once in a while they invited neighboring couples over for an evening, or went to their homes and had a wonderful time.

Three months after her marriage, a movie company announced that Carol had signed to appear in the first of several films. This first one was called "Snow White and the Three Stooges." In the fall Carol went to Hollywood to begin making it, and studying lessons in acting.

Now she was a movie star. But when the movie was finished, all she wanted was to return to Akron, to the home she was so proud of, and the man she loved.

Sometimes she is asked: "Do you ever regret having to work so hard so many years to win your Olympic medal?"

Carol shakes her head. "Mother made the right decisions," she smiles. "I don't regret a minute of the hard work I have put into skating. If something isn't worth working for, it is not worth very much. And hard work keeps you young and vital."

"Will you miss being at the Olympics in 1964?" they ask Carol.

Her eyes twinkle. "Who knows, I *might* be there," she says, and when they look surprised she laughs. "Not to skate myself," she says. "Of course I can't do that now that I have turned professional. But I am hoping there will be another Heiss there—my sister Nancy. And I will be there cheering her on."

The skating world hopes that Nancy *will* be at the winter Olympics in 1964. It has its eyes on her and on the family that tries to make "Heiss" equal to "Ice." Carol has aready done this. Nancy is winning for herself. And young Bruce is making his mark, too.

Three Olympic champions in one family? Why not? Perhaps this is just what will happen in the great years of sport that lie ahead.

Carol's deep personal happiness has always come from
joy of doing well and of caring for those around her

92

Parker, Robert
  AUTHOR

Carol Heiss, Olympic queen
  TITLE

92

Parker, Robert

Carol Heiss, Olympic queen

This book may be kept

FOURTEEN

A fine will be charged for each d   time.

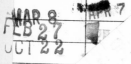

MAR 8   APR 7

FEB 27

OCT 22

NOV 8

NOV